T0204175

ARCTIC WOLF PACK VS. POLAR BEAR

BY NATHAN SOMMER

BELLWETHER MEDIA • MINNEAPOLIS, MN

Torque brims with excitement
perfect for thrill-seekers of all kinds.
Discover daring survival skills, explore
uncharted worlds, and marvel at mighty
engines and extreme sports. In *Torque* books,
anything can happen. Are you ready?

This edition first published in 2025 by Bellwether Media, Inc.

No part of this publication may be reproduced in whole or in part without
written permission of the publisher.
For information regarding permission, write to Bellwether Media, Inc.,
Attention: Permissions Department,
6012 Blue Circle Drive, Minnetonka, MN 55343.

Library of Congress Cataloging-in-Publication Data

LC record for Arctic Wolf Pack vs. Polar Bear available at:
https://lccn.loc.gov/2024019767

Editor: Suzane Nguyen   Designer: Hunter Demmin

Printed in the United States of America, North Mankato, MN.

TABLE OF CONTENTS

THE COMPETITORS 4

SECRET WEAPONS..................10

ATTACK MOVES 16

READY, FIGHT!.........................20

GLOSSARY..............................22

TO LEARN MORE......................23

INDEX 24

THE COMPETITORS

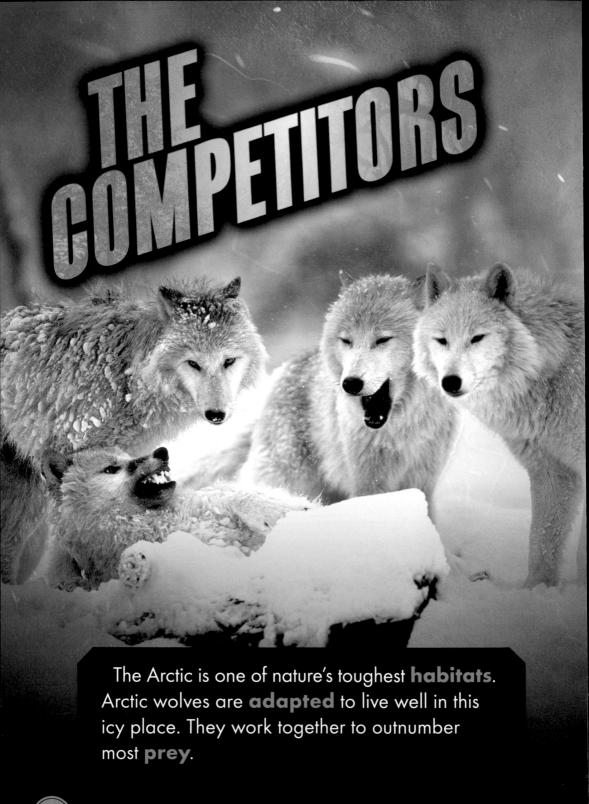

The Arctic is one of nature's toughest **habitats**. Arctic wolves are **adapted** to live well in this icy place. They work together to outnumber most **prey**.

The wolves share a home with polar bears. These **apex predators** use strength and size to hunt whatever they want. Which predator really rules the Arctic?

Arctic wolves have white fur and bushy tails. Large, padded paws and two thick coats help them survive the frozen **tundra**.

Arctic wolves are found in parts of Alaska, Canada, and Greenland. The wolves often make dens in caves or rock formations. They live in packs of around four to seven members.

CHANGING FUR

Arctic wolves are born with dark fur. Their fur turns white in their first year of life.

ARCTIC WOLF PROFILE

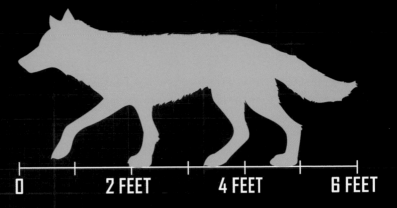

0   2 FEET   4 FEET   6 FEET

LENGTH
UP TO 6 FEET
(1.8 METERS)

WEIGHT
UP TO 154 POUNDS
(70 KILOGRAMS)

HABITATS

TUNDRA

ICE FIELDS

GLACIER VALLEYS

ARCTIC WOLF RANGE

■ RANGE

POLAR BEAR PROFILE

HEIGHT
ABOUT 8 FEET
(2.4 METERS)
ON BACK LEGS

8 FEET

6 FEET

4 FEET

WEIGHT
ABOUT 1,600 POUNDS
(726 KILOGRAMS)

2 FEET

HABITATS

TUNDRA   COLD OCEAN   ICE FLOES

POLAR BEAR RANGE

 RANGE

Polar bears are the world's largest land **carnivores**. They stand around 8 feet (2.4 meters) tall. They weigh up to 1,600 pounds (726 kilograms). The bears have long necks and bodies. Their fur is thick and white.

Polar bears are **solitary** animals. They often live near Arctic sea ice and coastal waters.

SECRET WEAPONS

TOP SPEED

20
10   30
0   40

40 MILES (64 KILOMETERS) PER HOUR

ARCTIC WOLF

20
10   30
0   40

28 MILES (45 KILOMETERS) PER HOUR

FASTEST HUMAN

Arctic wolves hunt in packs. They howl to tell pack members that prey is near. Then, they work together to chase prey. Some wolves run up to 40 miles (64 kilometers) per hour. Many animals cannot outrun these predators.

Large, furry paws help polar bears move on ice. Rough bumps on their feet help them **grip** the ice. The bears can move quickly without slipping.

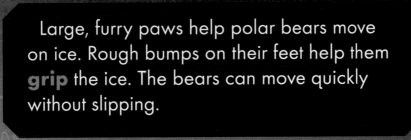

SUPER SWIMMERS

Webbed front paws help polar bears to be excellent swimmers. Some can swim for long distances without stopping!

Arctic wolves have strength in numbers.
Pack members surround their prey to scare it.
They work together to defeat much larger prey.

POLAR BEAR CLAW

2 INCHES
(5 CENTIMETERS)

Polar bears have strong, razor-sharp claws. The bears use their 2-inch-long (5-centimeter-long) claws to capture prey. They also use their claws to move on snow and ice.

SECRET WEAPONS

SPEED

TEAMWORK

POWERFUL JAWS

Arctic wolves have powerful jaws. Their jaws have 42 sharp teeth. Multiple bites can defeat most prey. They can even bite off large chunks of meat.

SECRET WEAPONS

LARGE, FURRY PAWS   STRONG, SHARP CLAWS   STRONG BITE

Polar bears have the strongest **bite force** of all bears. Their deadly bites have 1,200 pounds per square inch of force. This helps them easily snatch prey out of water.

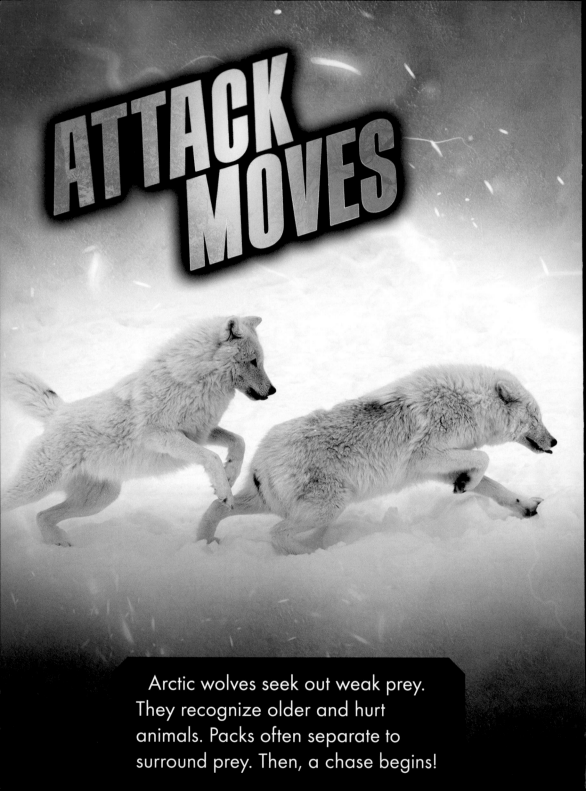

ATTACK MOVES

Arctic wolves seek out weak prey. They recognize older and hurt animals. Packs often separate to surround prey. Then, a chase begins!

Polar bears mostly hunt seals. These **ambush hunters** wait near holes in the ice where seals come up for air. Then, the bears capture them! Some polar bears dig young seals right out of the snow.

NOT PICKY

Polar bears eat whatever they can find. They will eat garbage and dead animals if they have to.

Arctic wolves chase prey until it gets tired. Their combined bites and attacks bring prey down. Packs share their meals after successful hunts.

MAJOR APPETITES

Arctic wolves can eat up to 20 pounds (9 kilograms) of food at once!

Polar bears chase prey at speeds of up to 25 miles (40 kilometers) per hour. They attack prey with sharp claws and deadly bites. One bite to the neck can defeat most animals.

READY, FIGHT!

An Arctic wolf pack circles a baby polar bear. The pack prepares to attack the baby bear. Suddenly, the baby's mother charges forward!

The wolves come together to bite the mother bear. She swipes several wolves with her sharp claws. The hurt wolf pack runs away. No one comes for this polar bear's baby!

GLOSSARY

adapted—well suited due to changes over a long period of time

ambush hunters—animals that sit and wait to catch their prey

apex predators—animals at the top of the food chain that are not preyed upon by other animals

bite force—the strength of an animal's bite

carnivores—animals that only eat meat

grip—to tightly hold

habitats—the homes or areas where animals prefer to live

prey—animals that are hunted by other animals for food

solitary—related to living alone

tundra—a flat, treeless area where the ground is always frozen

TO LEARN MORE

AT THE LIBRARY

Downs, Kieran. *Polar Bear vs. Walrus*. Minneapolis, Minn.: Bellwether Media, 2022.

Hudak, Heather C. *Wolf, Coyote, and Other Packs*. New York, N.Y.: Crabtree Publishing, 2023.

Stine, Megan. *Where Is the North Pole?* New York, N.Y.: Penguin Random House, 2022.

ON THE WEB

FACTSURFER

Factsurfer.com gives you a safe, fun way to find more information.

1. Go to www.factsurfer.com

2. Enter "Arctic wolf pack vs. polar bear" into the search box and click 🔍.

3. Select your book cover to see a list of related web sites.

INDEX

adapted, 4

apex predators, 5

Arctic, 4, 5, 9

attacks, 18, 19, 20

bites, 14, 15, 18, 19, 20

bodies, 9

carnivores, 9

chase, 16, 18, 19

claws, 13, 19, 20

coats, 6

colors, 6, 9

dens, 6

feet, 11

food, 17, 18

fur, 6, 9, 11

habitats, 4, 6, 7, 8

hunt, 5, 10, 17, 18

ice, 4, 9, 11, 13, 17

jaws, 14

packs, 6, 10, 12, 16, 18, 20

paws, 6, 11

prey, 4, 10, 12, 13, 14, 15, 16, 17, 18, 19

range, 6, 7, 8

size, 5, 7, 8, 9, 13

snow, 13, 17

solitary, 9

speed, 10, 19

swimmers, 11

tails, 6

teeth, 14

waters, 9, 15

weapons, 14, 15

The images in this book are reproduced through the courtesy of: Marques, front cover (polar bear); oliver magritzer, front cover (Arctic wolf); karlumbriaco, pp. 2-3, 6-7, 20-24; GUDKOV ANDREY, pp. 2-3, 20-24; 4FR, p. 4; isabel kendzior, p. 5; Jane Rix, pp. 8-9; Michal Ninger, p. 10; Chase D'animulls, p. 11; Glass and Nature, p. 12; imageBROKER.com GmbH & Co. KG / Alamy Stock Photo/ Alamy, p. 13; Vladimir Gramagin, p. 14; Mircea Costina, p. 14 (speed); Ondrej Chvatal, p. 14 (teamwork); Holger Kirk, p. 14 (powerful jaws); Andyworks, p. 15; Heather M Davidson, p. 15 (large, furry paws); James_Robert, p. 15 (strong, sharp claws); Nagel Photography, p. 15 (strong bite); Jim Cumming, p. 16; karenfoleyphotography, p. 17; Mircea Costina, p. 18; GTW, pp. 2-3, 19, 20-24.